Last One Out

LAST ONE OUT

Poems by
Ernest Hilbert

Measure Press
Evansville, Indiana

The text of this book is composed in Baskerville.
Composition by R.G.
Manufacturing by Ingram.

Cover photograph by Matthew Wright, © 2019
Author photograph by Richard Malouf, © 2015
Jacket design consultant Leah Giovannoli

Last One Out contains mature themes. Discretion is advised for readers under the age of 40.

Hilbert, Ernest
  Last One Out / by Ernest Hilbert — 1st ed.

  ISBN-13: 978-1-939574-29-9
  ISBN-10: 1-939574-29-3
  Library of Congress Control Number: 2018968612

Measure Press
526 S. Lincoln Park Dr.
Evansville, IN 47714
http://www.measurepress.com/measure/

Acknowledgements

The author extends warmest gratitude to the editors of the publications in which these poems originally appeared, some in different forms, including *Academic Questions* (National Association of Scholars), *American Arts Quarterly*, *American Journal of Poetry*, *American Poet* (Academy of American Poets), *Asheville Poetry Review*, *Barrow Street*, *Battersea Review*, *Boston Review*, *Clarion* (Boston Poetry Union), *Connotation Press: An Online Artifact*, *The Dark Horse*, *Drunken Boat*, *Edinburgh Review*, *Fruita Pulp*, *Hopkins Review*, *Horizon Review*, *Jacket*, *Literary Imagination*, *Literary Matters*, *Measure*, *Meridian*, *Modern Drunkard*, *The New Criterion*, *The New Republic*, *Oxonian Review*, *Parnassus*, *Per Contra*, *Philadelphia Inquirer*, *Pleiades*, *Plume*, *Poetry Northeast*, *Raintown Review*, *Sewanee Review*, *Smartish Pace*, *Southwest Review*, *Think Journal*, *Verse*, *Vocabula Review*, and *The Yale Review*.

"Mars Ultor" appeared in *Best American Poetry 2018*, published by Scribner, a division of Simon & Schuster. It was also included in the protest anthology *Donald Trump: The Magazine of Poetry*. The following poems appeared in the chapbook *Aim Your Arrows at the Sun*, LATR Editions, New York City, in an edition of 250 copies, hand-sewn, in letterpress wrappers: "On Passing the Remains of a T-62 in the Sinai," "At the 100th Anniversary of the Antiquarian Booksellers Association at the Royal Geographical Society," "Haunts," "Aim Your Arrows at the Sun," "Bread and Circuses," "As the Lost Kings Uphold My Side," "Dining with Representatives of the Vatican Museum," "Surrender of Breda," and "Disasters of War." "Great White Fleet" and "In Memory of a Writer" were reprinted in *The Best of The Raintown Review: 2010-2015*. "The Haywain" appeared on the website *Poetry Daily*.

"Against the Art of War" originally appeared in a letterpress edition *Against the Art of War*, published by Temporary Culture, with three tipped-in aquatint etchings by London-based Canadian artist Judith Clute and an additional anti-war poem by Henry Wessells, printed by David Wolfe of Portland, Maine, hand-bound in paste-paper boards, in an edition of 26 lettered copies, signed by the authors and the artist, and five numbered copies reserved for artist, authors, and printer. Institutional collections holding copies of the book include the Lilly Library (Indiana University), Rubenstein Library (Duke University), the Beinecke Library (Yale University), and Poets House in New York City.

"My Father's Dante" was selected as a Laureates' Choice for the 2016 Maria W. Faust Sonnet Contest. "Rowing in the Dawn" appeared in 2014 as a limited-edition full-color broadside from Lithic Press in Colorado. "Martini" appeared as a signed limited-edition broadside designed by artist Jessica Tanny and issued by the Cambridge Public Library on the occasion of Ernest Hilbert's reading there on November 13th, 2014, in an edition of 60 numbered copies, 1-10 signed by author, artist, and promoter Daniel Wuenschel, 11-25 signed by Hilbert only, 26-40 and 51-60 unsigned, and 41-50 signed by Hilbert exclusively for subscribers, including the Woodberry Poetry Room at Harvard University.

"Haunts," recorded by Danielle Fox, aired twice on WHYY FM, Philadelphia's NPR Station, 90.9 MHz, as part of a National Poetry Month feature on Morning Edition, hosted by Jennifer Lynn, on Tuesday, April 24th, 2018. "Kingsessing Avenue" appeared as part of the City of Philadelphia Office of Arts, Culture and the Creative Economy's "Write Your Block" project, documenting Philadelphia neighborhoods. A recording of "Walnut Street" was broadcast on Georgia State Radio, WRAS 88.5 FM, and its affiliates on May 1st, 2015 as part of the program "Locals Only: Philly."

The epigraph to chapter three is from the Anglo-Saxon poem known as "The Wanderer," which appears in *Codex Exoniensis* or *The Exeter Book*. It may be translated as "Where is the giver of treasure? / Where are the places at the feast? / Where are the celebrations in the hall?" *Non Omnis Moriar* appears in Horace's *Carmina* 3/30:6 and may be translated as "I shall not wholly die."

My deepest thanks go out to my wife Lynn and our son Ian, my family and friends, the staff of Measure Press, my colleagues, and everyone who has supported me over the years. *Last One Out* owes its life to careful readings by Nicholas Friedman, David Yezzi, Justin Quinn, and Bill Coyle.

For My Father

CONTENTS

1.

2.

3.

4.

5.

6.

7.

Non Omnis Moriar

1.

. . . as the good gardener seasons his soil by sundry sorts of compost: as muck or marl, clay or sand, and many times by blood or lees of oil or wine, or stale, or perchance with more costly drugs: and waters his plants, and weeds his herbs or flowers, and prunes his branches, and unleaves his boughs to let in the sun: and twenty other ways cherisheth them, and cureth their infirmities, and so makes that never or very seldom any of them miscarry, but bring forth their flowers and fruits in season.

— George Puttenham

Welcome to all the Pleasures

The wind was wasp and pollen,
Charred pork and dragonfly.

My grandfather — German
With shoulders of granite,

Of beer and blue skies,
Blast furnaces — grew impatient

When he learned that, at four,
I'd still not learned to swim.

He hoisted me in summer air,
Spun me out over

The sluggish murk and let go.
I swear the river had no bottom.

I smacked the sun-fierce surface
With a sharp cold crash,

Then silence and stunned slowness.
I finned and swung,

Hung between what glows above
And what pulls below.

Yggdrasil

A Bach cantata slurs to static
On the stereo as a hurricane
Rumbles through our attic.

Barrages of quicksilver rain
Machine-gun aluminum.
Darkness drags around the lawn.

By afternoon, skies foam
To white. Air is washed clean.
The bright grass is strewn

With debris like a battle scene.
We round the house to discover
The chimney down, but intact,

Like some primitive ziggurat.
We kick leaves, find a pool cover,
Plastic bags, limbs storm-cracked,

Spilled out like roasted bird-flesh with twists of fat.
A TV aerial needles up like the mast
Of a wrecked schooner. Beyond it,

We find the tilted apple tree.
What appeared, in the past,
So permanent is now split

Down the middle, pulled free
From its base by the storm.
Lumps of sweating soil spread

Where dendritic root protrudes into
Damp air, the tree's capillary form
Capsized, not entirely dead,

But dying by parts where it grows.
A truck and great chain will haul
It from this earth, leave a hole

We'll someday fill, a socket of mud
Where our tree once seemed so tall,
Now a den black like a vein of coal

Or splash of parched ancestral blood.

As the Lost Kings Uphold My Side

My broad oak desk is darkened like a lost
King's blade-scored, beer-soaked table at the head
Of a candled mead hall in winter hills.
My hair is a hammered golden helmet,
My shirt, a bright shower of silver mail.
I tilt back the glass. The cubes
Throw out a bronze flare and clink.
The cigarette smoke rises and trembles
From the last of a burned village.
My cats stalk the shadowed corners
Of the room like slow, muscular cougars
On the snow-conquered walls of a ruin.

Recessional

My father would leave the salt-encrusted Ford
Unlocked, the only car in the winter lot,
And draw a key for the heavy church door.

He'd click on a light over the organ,
Where it glowed in black like an angler fish
At the entrance to a cavern on the ocean floor.

His eyeglasses lit white from the bulb,
Bearded, he eased his bulk onto the bench,
Rifling folders of music in manuscript.

The huge old organ rumbled chorales,
Roared enormous chords, stopping midway
Through a passage, consigning a long resonance

From transept into the beamed vault of the nave,
Over the stone angel that shouldered the lectern
And silver vases emptied of fern and tulip.

In towering stained glass, lead outlines of Apostles
And The Ascension, lakes of green and violet, bright
In morning light, rose blackened and cryptic.

I explored while he scribbled notes on the sheets,
At times a subtle oath or cheerful *"ha!"*
While working up his Bach arrangements.

In a moment of boredom before the looming pulpit
I saw that a boy as small as I could easily
Pass clear under the polished wooden pews.

Never before would I have been so low
To the floor and childlike, not at services
With the adults. It felt like a discovery.

I inched on my dusty belly under the cold pews,
Slipping from the safe gloom thrown by his light
Toward the deep and promising darkness.

Memorial Days

The park's in bloom, its gate seeping honeysuckle.
I work to shed some flab I gained last winter.
It's a year since I spoke at my father's grave

Before bayonets and brass bands for his memorial.
Twenty-four years of loss I had to disinter
And put back again with a smile and a wave.

I can hardly remember what I thought or said.
My gravity's art weakens and uncoils.
Eased, what was caught to my orbit drifts.

I slough skin and clip nails, scrub iron pans of fat,
Pick up blue Doritos bags, purple soda cans,
Some disorder obvious, some imperceptible.

I keep too many books   some his, half still unread,
My house a vault piled up with pointless spoils,
Acquired or passed down, some stolen, or gifts.

What's in them? Hearts and wars, cities knocked flat,
My father's marks, lists, sketches, small plans,
Lives that in time became impossible.

Sing We

Berry-plump, the bees bungle through sparse grass.
They ride cool gusts, eddy around me
As I cradle a guitar at my father's stone
This spring afternoon. Shadows of boughs mass
And sweep the lichened epitaph. Pine cones
Are piled in needle patches beneath the tree.
The swarm spares me. It knows I've been
Through enough. Its golds emblazon the grays
And worn-out browns. An impudent black fly
Alights again and again on my hand. I pin
It with my palm, then let it go. It stays
With me and lands again. Blocking the sky,
Sentries of Weymouth Pine drain glittering old
Wounds down furrowed sides pearled like mold.
I strum a jumble of chords, but they will not
Resolve to songs I long ago forgot.

Two Portraits

Two portraits lean on their stands and watch me.
The first frame, stained dark cherry, nicked pink
At its edges, clasps Dürer's engraving,
"St. Jerome in his Study." The bearded saint,
Bald and intent, gazes down on his own work,
Never aware of me, as a dog and human-
Faced lion doze beside his slippers.
The image's coppery scintilla comfort me.

Light breaks from his pate like a borealis,
Serene as the light through his window.
The glass becomes a pool that swims
With reflected light, his study rippled under
Clear water, near enough, almost, to touch,
Like a drowned royal grave filled with sparks
And traces of an imagined world.

The other frame, cheap rusted metal, cocked,
Holds a fading black-and-white photograph
Of my father, raising me, a blond boy
Before a piano and a long board
Chalked with staves: Old melodies and high notes,
A wall of trills and delicate runes
On the antechamber of an ancient tomb.

The notes run up and up from left to right
Disappearing behind the great bear-form
Of my bearded father in striped tie and tweed.

He cups his big hands beneath my small legs.
Through his glasses — they reflect
The room and hide his eyes —
He watches me at my work.

Dimming in time, depths flattened,
The portrait shines like a coffin set on end,
Still empty of its intended occupant.

My Father's Dante

You were gone twenty years before I read
The book that draws me faster on to you.
The world you left got worse, and crowded too,
Charon capsized by cargoes of new dead.
I'm midway gone, in a grim winter mood,
Pinned by all I did, instead of what I could.
Among the lessons I failed till now to learn
Is that, however handsome or witty,
We should expect to receive no pity.
We hurt as much from what we half-forget
As from the things we carefully conserve.
You say: There is so much more to observe.
We will descend, and see, and not regret
That we fall, we shiver — we shine and burn.

Ship Bottom, 1972

The photo's since softened to amber,
Holding light like honey, its colors, long ago
Drawn from trees, aged in the intervening
Years by acids in the air. I remember:
The sun-hot sand, whitecaps that glint and grow,
Climbing to a brilliant crash. You're leaning
And smiling over me, a blond boy, my hair
Lit like gold at noon, your dawn-red hair held
By a kerchief of forest and deep-sea blue —
You are beautiful, and we are a pair,
And I am still with you, embraced between
Spring and winter in the eternal and true
Summer, autumn always coming on,
You, forever there, smiling with your son.

Great Bay Estuary

Chuckling gulls luft up to swipe and hang
In muggy air over the riverside's
Deadfall — jagged white as a splintered ice-flow.
A tern goes and returns like a boomerang
Across the scene. An Eastern Kingbird glides
Beside a dock cemented with guano.

The dock's slats tilt down, disappearing at the end
To rot in slow water. Nearer, a marsh wren
Sways on a thorny stem. From the northwest,
Curving along the broad river's bend,
The startled dart of a fierce-winged merlin,
Scouting out or returning to its nest.

Four decades ago I plied these waters
With my father — he at the helm, running
In early haze between black-tar banks:
"Jibe ho!" — the aluminum boom swings as my father's
Hand draws the tiller, the wake's V following —
A metal rattle as my father cranks

The winch — the thrill of holding on as we heel
And the sideways world is wind and bulrush,
Ghosts of petrified white cedars standing
Apart out in the endless mud, our keel
Roiling the black bottom. In the murky hush
Of dusk, we arrive at the familiar landing . . . .

Beyond the sandy downstream knolls, behold
A summer flotilla of tundra swans.
In strobing depths beneath the broken dock,
Elegant Venetian galleys of gold-
Finned pickerel row through rays to bronze,
White perch arrowing silver around a rock

To the sun-ruled surface where stratocumuli
Loom in to warn of an advancing storm.
A sad and majestic eastern red cedar
Bushes over the brown current, berry
Clusters dusty-blue, a funerary form
Leaning to its mirror in the lessening light.

Fires smolder, far off. The ancient rough-shield
Shell of a diamondback terrapin bobs
On a soaked log sideways in the slow stream.
Scum from brackish water dims its battlefield
Polish. All that floats here — flaked bark, knobs
Of old limbs, cola cans — drawn as if in a dream

Toward the Great Bay and the sea beyond.
I lie in bed under cresting waves of wool,
Steering my ivory sloop with sails of ice
In the New Jersey sunset — a reed my wand;
Its tufts a dirty, living gold — the pull
Of memory, time-consumed sinking of sights

Once solid. The stars are out already,
And I go down where swamps sieve water shed
By the pine-stands and tangled low scrub, a sight
That gathers around the cloud-flood horizon — I see
Everything, all around, going red a while, led
To my bedside in the last of the light.

2.

I'm the king, sitting in the dark . . .
        — Celtic Frost, "Jewel Throne"

Rowing in the Dawn

1.
We heave the great oak hull over our heads,
Lower it into the dark off the dock.
Oars clunk into brass oarlocks. Latches clink shut.
We push off past the soft black velvet
Of barge chains swathed in river moss.
Our blades, bearing St. Catherine's cutting wheel,
Catch and lug us forward into the dark.
Our knock-hard longboat divides the river.
We're Venetian oarsmen, Egyptian pullers,
Athenian shoulders raising speed to ram.
Cold wind fans Hard Shield-Ferns in the meadows,
Dips slender thistle, courses through stone walls
As freezing chalk curls through the granite sky.

2.
Swans, stirred from invisible stillness,
Lunge at our prow, as if to assault us.
At the last yard, they pad and splash up
From the empty Isis and soar
Into the thinning darkness above us.
We pull and watch our milky wake.

3.

The moon withers over limestone,
And from the night emerge the reaching edges
Of English elms, silver birches, star sedge,
Aspens, ashes, and alders. Beyond,
Sashed in retreating lunar mist, the spires,
The bell tower, and, beneath it, the priory
Wrecked by Norse maulers in the departed dark,
Venetian façades clung with red ivy,
Norman chevrons enclosed by barbs of holly.

Kingsessing Avenue

The men sift the ash of an incinerated Victorian
For the clink of coin or cufflink,
Some remnant in the wreckage
One might don or exchange once more.

Embers of dandelion
Are dimmed as the slow breeze spreads
Soot along the block, to porches, sills,
Soft gray clovers of cats' paws.

Haunts

A clear sky over Kingsessing Avenue:
Iron gates catch a trove of wind-blown foil,
Crushed cupolas of Styrofoam,
Folded sails of wet newspaper.

Charles Addams, you strolled
These streets, observed the late sun
Burn and bulge in bay windows,
Sketched mansards on misty Sundays.

Would you have drawn me, peering
From behind blinds, edged by columns
Under a cornice jeweled with raindrops,
As sun returns long shadows to our street?

Center City

A bank was here. Shadow letters remain
Like damp squares of towels peeled from concrete.

Sparse-whiskered kids, their dogs leashed with frayed twine,
Clumsily strum chords on untuned guitars.

They recline and squint, puff roll-ups,
Fatigues worn at the knee, black boots broken.

Their hounds sniff and plead with watery eyes
At mute passersby. Urine pools in a corner.

In scattered groups, like aimless parts
Of a convoy attacked from the air,

The motley, medieval jamboree
Swells day by day and gets rowdier.

Above it, three flagpoles angle out like
Antennae, feeling the city's mulled

Humidity for a message. One small
American flag flaps like a half-empty sail.

Walnut Street

I dodge down the crowded July street,
Breathing garbage and humid perfume.
The stifling block is wild at noon.
Stores prop open doors to lure in buyers:
Banks of icy air waft out in columns,
And I cross through one and nearly shiver.

As I emerge again to warmth,
I remember swimming in cedar lakes
That flashed like dirty tin in summer,
Buoyed in greasy tea-stained water.
We kicked to keep afloat near the adults,
Then raced past the roped orange markers.

The lifeguard's whistle pierced our splashes.
Undercurrents from freezing springs gushed
On our bellies, then sun-kettled eddies, then cold,
Paddling and lunging for those small islands
That seemed to recede with each breathless lash
Of our arms through the churned, cloudy water.

Strung

My taut hammock is cradle and litter,
First and final transport of the season,
Meshwork hove and bent to obey my weight.

A tickling sting calls down a careless slap,
Then another, and more. I am besieged
Until my arms are smeared with insect parts.

They are ancient, first-made, and fast. I am
Outweaponed, prey to thirsting brigandage,
My blood pooled freely among their squadrons.

I may slaughter them, being weightier,
A willful mortal centered in my web,
But they spin away loaded with black cargo,

A rich salt relieved from my poked-through skin,
Launched and spun in sunshine as if I weighed
Nothing and earth was never built below.

Amusements

These are the long days that fill with night
As an amusement park goes silver, pink, and gold.
The chimes still lure the crowds through a hazy glow
To the Haunted House, the Tunnel of Love.
The mallet thumps hard and clangs the bell.
And here, the roller coaster looms above,
Brightly-painted cars in endless ascent.
The line, longer than it seemed, wends to snake
Around the bend to the clicking, cold stile
And the seat that will pull you so high you can view
The landscape all around as if it were new —
Fields, lakes, and freeways, spread below a moment,
Then the clinking slows as you reach the top
And panic, knowing you can't make it stop.

At the 100th Anniversary of the Antiquarian Booksellers Association at the Royal Geographical Society

Black cabs slow to ranks before Lowther Lodge.
Lord Markham appears to doze, looks drowsily
From his marble recess to Bayswater
And the Serpentine, undaunted, ignored.

Jagger's bronze Shackleton is thick-bundled.
He looms heavily like an armored saint.
He seems to squint for snow, yearn for blizzards,
So he might again prove himself helpful.

A woman, tipsy, snags her blue silk gown
In the cab's door as her husband fumbles
With his defiant tie. With others, they crunch
Onto the interior courtyard's gravel.

The smiling chancellor, with a glinting gold
Shard of champagne aloft in his hand,
Calls for silence, and affable *shushes* spread
Like the last steam from an ancient engine.

An award is presented, and a small
Bespectacled man blushes, ever redder,
As he attempts to address the slipping crowd
From the top of the stairs. He coughs. Then blinks.

His voice ebbs in the breeze. Cell phones chirp.
Airliners roar overhead. Pigeons startle themselves.
Buses rasp down Kensington Gore. Whispers
Float up, and sports cars honk brass hunting horns.

His lips move for a while. He gestures dreamily
With his silver prize, his wife looking on,
And the sun burns through marble clouds,
Pools the rims of his glasses with mercury.

3.

Hwær cwom maþþumgyfa?
Hwær cwom symbla gesetu?
Hwær sindon seledreamas?
　　　　　　— *Codex Exoniensis*

Chelsea Hotel

I'm an awkward X
On stormed sheets.

My Roman tie
Is trampled silk

Of Adriatic sunrise.
Its molten foil

Plunges in my chest.
I sit up in the dark.

I listen to Bach
And sulk.

I sink all night
Through the sun.

The hard sky
Is cold clear blue.

It holds a heavy glass glow
As I roll into black.

Cabs bank and coast
Down crazed straits below.

The floor slides
Like a raft in a tide.

The walls groan
And creak with whalesong.

We made love here,
Face down in a summer

River for hours,
Pulled toward

Softening surf
Of a warmer ocean.

Snow-rigged galleons
Of cloud curl apart

Far above the city.
They perish and astound.

I am a barbarian king brooding
In long captivity.

I digest
Whole forests and their deer.

The gaped ghost O
Of neon

Over the iron balustrade
Fills the room.

My heart is a meteorite.
I am its crater.

Tutorial

When you've got no looks to lose,
You won't worry about losing them.

If you've got no taste for booze,
You won't feel bad from boozing.

If you get no inheritance,
You'll have nothing to squander.

Unburdened, there is less to burn,
No load to lean under, no grace to learn.

Memory of a Writer

We tell stories that will last forever.
You don't have to believe that. It's okay.
Still, we hear notes from a song, far off somewhere,
Though we can only make out its crude contours,
And after a while of quietly straining
To hear it, we just let it fade away,
Like jet trails across a chilled blue sky,
Blue like a cheap drink on some holiday
We never took, but we know others did,
Must have, while we gathered here in this room
Laddered with shelves, bricked-in with books,
Telling stories about things that may
Have happened, and often did, somewhere else.

Advice

When one is absent
The others won't miss her.
We give attention
To the one we see.

When he's off,
He's through. You talk
To the one next to you,
Note the newly arrived.

Once gone, hearts seem
To grow fonder,
But only of the cruder
Outline left behind.

They are less fond
Of the bundle
Of difficulties
And dullness that fills

Back in when the welcome
Has worn again.
You may solve this
By appearing

To be everywhere
At once, but,
In the end, you'll be
Nowhere ever again.

Martini

1.
The ice is drenched in the silver cylinder
With Bluecoat, vermouth, the juice of pickled peppers.

The splash tingles the cubes. They crack and fuse.
I rest it to chill, stir, then shower loose

A tidy rain to fill the glass chalice.
It glows on my lips like afternoon air.

2.
Solemn ceremony of president,
Executive, and, after all, the poet,

A clear, terrible fuel, rite of the WASP,
American legend, birthright, bequest:

Supreme distraction, long ago, for a time
Of polio, smallpox, economic decline;

Then back for the Cold War, to melt away
The edge on the Age of Anxiety

When the Atom Bomb made sobriety's
Appeal pale beside a cold stem of Gilbey's.

3.
We scarcely stop to think, night and day,
Yet still the true, indisputable way

To rinse cerebral soot is to simply say
"Dry, please, and a little dirty." It's okay

To soak there in the rich, swabbed ambience
After a day of cubicle fluorescence

And go a bit numb at nerve ends, a sense
Of drowning in place, serenely. So dispense

Wisdom and foolishness with a lemon twist
That shines like a hot coil above the wrist;

Or royal rust of a salt-defused mine,
The olive remote in its foggy brine.

Glass of Absinthe

New Orleans

Decisions are uncomfortable
In this atmosphere. Valves drain, swell to ballad —

Measures pound flaked light, sun over
Iron lace of a railing on Royal Street —

Metal scrolled into oak leaves, acorns, sad long horns
In the day's shadows — urinal smell, late coffee.

A life shaped by digressions: Linger long
Enough, and death might move somewhere else.

She seems drunk but is not, her white skirt webbed
With black from a fall on wet cobblestones.

Nothing is simple. There is no good news.
She lights a small cigarette. She nods off.

She drinks up. She moves on. The horns stop, sprawl,
Speed up. Snares salvo in the scorched dark.

The Haywain

Bosch's demons, roosting
Against the luminous sky
Of the Low Countries, emerge

Shaped of stone or dirty light —
Perched atop the haywain
Blowing long slender horns.

These jigging imps, eager
To guide peasants from their rustic
Scenery to another, unknowable one,

Are themselves missing or far
From a place that seems not
To have needed them so much

As their bounty, collected from
The breakable flesh of Europe.
Even in the soot-straked valleys

Of perdition on a triptych's flanking
Panel they dance in a different air.
Lodged into this bright world

Without permission. They exist
In the dusty glare and rabbled
Foreground as if for a briefest

Moment — or else all eternity,
Divided from true rhythms
Of a flowered world — dominion

Of conceit, toil, and tears —
Oblige the eye to grasp
More surely what truly belongs.

Ultramist Sport ™

The seared gold hull and Atlantic-blue spout
Bring to mind heat and young health. The greasy sheen
And cartoon tints of this tube of old sunscreen —
Kinked at center, cargo of clouds squeezed out —
Is flashy as a beach toy, bright as a sail,
And always soothing, like a Yacht Rock song.

It is a plastic promise, like a spade and pail,
Of days crossed out on calendars now long
Lost to damp floors of landfills. It summons —
Who knows how — hazy vistas, aromas of steak,
Sprinkler-shimmered lawns, stubbed toes, pour of sun's
Devastated diamonds on an icy lake.

I think of the tube interred in a drawer
Cluttered with dulled razors, deodorant stumps,
Two sun-bleached beach badges once worn,
A brush's thicket of bristles with clumps
Of lost hair. In its candy shell, the lotion
Pledges protection from stings of steep light.

It dreams like a bay in the humid night,
Still promising summers already gone.

Last One Out

Some lied to get away from their own friends,
And he always said that so much of it depends . . .

One day, the last host will slam the last door,
The last smoked ash will settle on the floor,

And he'll look up, and stop, maybe toast
Himself, with the slow, confused motions of a ghost.

4.

Those trees in whose dim shadow
The ghastly priest doth reign
The priest who slew the slayer,
And shall himself be slain.
— Thomas Macaulay

Mars Ultor

Before they had a fleet
Romans rowed on logs
As they prepared to meet

Carthage. Treaties, public
Or secret, do little when
The border of the republic

Is breached without notice:
More tug of war
Than elegant chess.

Some ask: Is *virtù* virtue?
After reconciliation, consensus,
Appeasement, the coup.

Some rely on law,
But law relies on guns,
Or must withdraw.

Brutes push their way to power,
But the muddiest barbarian
Also wants the throne an hour,

And dons a crown, marks affairs,
Nods under a golden branch until
A stronger one turns up the stairs.

Disasters of War

Goya

It is September, and I lunch in rain.
I do not like your city. I do not

Welcome the filling sky as I once could.
I notice nothing, however fatal,

In the foreground. I discard those ballads
Devoted to empire and disaster.

I belong among the hanged, whose ladders
Have drawn back at last, who slow the wind.

I belong among sources of etchings
And illumination. I too belong

Among what follows, is again ample,
Unruly, the suffering that becomes

Easier to record when it belongs
To another. I wander for concord

And clarity. I have learned little yet,
And remember less. I miss my red cat

Centering himself on my books to sleep.
I miss the world calculated and small.

I want nothing of boulevards, fast food,
And I am finished with the toll of the free

And dispensable. I miss my music,
My twilight and unlocking, and the past,

Where she will repeat "I am still singing.
The sky is ours. Wreck yourself here and stay."

On Passing the Remains of a T-62 in the Sinai

At a crossroad the armed escort
Slows. Gears grind down behind.
Here, a battalion paused too long,
Proof that armies advanced this far
In the baffling waste. Look at this
Drab tank, out farther than the rest,
As if to flee or perhaps press an attack,
Cased in deep armor but punctured.

The rockets that torched these hard husks
Left dark pinpoints. The tank's heavy as a dune,
Its patina matured to match neighboring rocks.
It looks like a crab washed onto sand,
Treads spun out from rows of barrel-like wheels,
Drive sprockets spiked stiff like sea urchins,
The hull of rolled steel, thick hatch flipped up,
Blasted open or lifted for escape . . . .

Another has lost its turtle-like turret,
A hollow half skull, dish for rare rainfall,
And one last, at an angle to the rest,

Its glacis plate sunk in sand, probing smoothbore
Angled down, as if to acknowledge
A long-ago blow and loss, and bow forever.

Leningrad

Seventh Symphony, Shostakovich

At last the stink of summer's siege sank away,
As mercury slid, vivid as new blood,
To the end of the thermometer's lance.
Our composer exhausts the day
On the conservatory roof, above mud
And tanks, listening as the slow advance
Of armies builds in time to a violent chord.
Horns blast open the city's snowy gate.
We boil horses and harness girls to tow
Corpses. The black boxes strung along wires
Urge us to the speaker's relentless wish.
Strings shriek and strafe. Tympani detonate.
The metronome swings dreamily, a sword
On the frozen plaza of piano,
Chandeliers shimmering like huge bonfires
In the evening of its iron polish.

Great White Fleet

White citadels melt into silhouettes,
Decks of fleece, big guns slimmed to flecks.
Their smoke thaws like frost warmed from a window,
Arrayed like combine harvesters on the plains.

Maine rests at anchor in Yokohama,
Ohio in Suez, Kansas at Gibraltar.

Memories gauzed by so much white,
These clockwork specters, beautifully built
For battle, powdery blurs, each towing
Its empty thoughts behind, paired like lovers
On their grand stereoscopic divide,
Great instruments diminished to snow.

Bread and Circuses

Juvenal

Surplus grains surge down immense flumes,
And wine decants down marble stairs.
We hardly notice now their ancient tombs,
But brace to inherit much newer cares.
One thinks *My Lord* to see on the TV:
A special report: "Help my fat *bay*by!"
It leans over like a tower of dough,
Tuber-fat fingers greasy from ground cow,
Vivacity of the innocent slurred.
On fenced plains, a head is culled from a herd.

Aim Your Arrows at the Sun

Beer suds slip back down the beer bottle's neck,
Bask in the den of dim light like frog spawn
On creek water, amber with softened sunlight.
Hornets spin over a nearby dumpster.
They dive for mold buttered on chicken carcasses
Like soap in the curve of a kitchen sink,

Semen sliding slowly down a bare leg,
A bowl poured full with fresh tapioca,
Scum on a toilet's porcelain gullet,
Foamy cream skimmed from an aluminum tub —
Silver moonlight glinting from its cold surface.
It leans into soft manure and yellow grass.

Surrender of Breda

Velázquez

An aristocratic Dane in tailored tweed, blond hair whisked to one
side, clunked a bottle of whiskey down on the desk, waved
his hand into the smoky air as if shooing a desert fly: "This
is so vulgar. It really is," meaning the Brahms *Festival Overture.*
For one flashing moment light glinted in the library window.

"The ocean will never cease to give us pleasure." She posed on
wet rocks against a distant storm; he stood beside a yawl
overturned beneath the seawall and complained: "My
friends, they either disappoint me or drive me to jealousy."

The way he discussed the more decadent Roman Emperors, one
almost thinks that he wished historical circumstances had
permitted him to speak of himself in such terms.

A letter arrived from the coast: "I just returned from a stroll. Here
are some thoughts. This time of year the gulls feed on the
juniper trees. They cannot perch on the branches because
the branches cannot support their weight, so they slowly flap
their wings to keep in place to eat the berries. It is beautiful,
this swaying."

And he asked: "What rivers, what air, are my men to cross?" The
enemy replied: "if you can give us seven laps across the
Hellespont, you may drown at your discretion. That was our
deal!"

Typed at a portable desk on the Normandy beachhead, beneath clouds of naval gunfire, bodies soaked in sand: "The wreckage is vast and startling."

Until the Sea above Us
Closed Again

You feel as if you're being stalked
Today and don't know who to trust.
Who splashed this wine across the floor?
We'd help if we could arrange it.

And what about that night you walked
Alone to work? And now you must
Stay home and sit and watch the door.
What's normal now the facts don't fit?

"The system cannot be unlocked.
Your password has expired and must
Be changed." "You must log in with your
Password in order to make a change."

Now, from behind, you see a man,
An open umbrella in the crook
Of his arm, hands unseen at his waist.
He faces between a brick wall and the back

Of a bin — Toys for Tots. You can
Watch him awhile. You have to look.
You realize the way they're placed
His hands are on . . . and now the black

Sky pours. He turns to you. A van
Stops. You know him, you think. The book
Hasn't started. You might be erased.
You're home. We know. Don't bother to pack.

5.

The older lives
Have no wish to be stood in
Rows or at right angles.

— W.H. Auden, "Ode to Gaea"

Glorious First

1.
Fireflies glide leisurely on the yard tonight,
Whirl of bullion, Will-o'-the-Wisp,
Soft-bodied constellations of cold light,
Brightening like beacons, dimming to eclipse.
They wash and signal in their delicate funnel,
Flashing silent broadsides at our porch.

2.
Each is an ignited and suddenly dampened torch
Torturing Leander, lost in his dark channel.

3.
Caravaggio daubed bright oils of milled
Firefly to light St. Matthew's angel on canvas.

4.
Boys flourish glass jars through the darkness
To imprison the fireflies. Once filled,
The jars swim like wind-stirred lanterns. Girls giggle
As they twist quivering wings into a hoop —
Fireflies, still alive, tremor and wriggle —
To fashion shimmering bracelets. They droop
As they die, but glow like mythic gold in mists,
Smears of troubled sunlight on innocent wrists.

Against the Art of War

1.
Is it merely the making and ending
Of states that justifies ceaseless sending
Of youthful armies each generation
　　　To patrol and maintain
　　　Uneasy peace, sustain
Alliance with our latest creation?

War begins and builds in all things.
With fears and fantasies it grows and brings
New goals and assurance of gain.
　　　We rear it. We claim it
　　　For our own and name it
The myth of Hercules, the mark of Cain.

2.
It waits all summer in the young wasp's tail,
　　　On a tetanus-bristling nail,
Abrasion of nipple against new-worn cloth,
　　　Flutter of kamikaze moth,

The ache and doubt of thirty-eight-hour birth,
　　　The glare of sunlight scorching earth,
The crouch and pounce of household cat,
　　　The loser's shoulders pinned to mat,

The slippery floor of the slaughterhouse,
    A trap pulled back for a mouse;
It's there in landslide and lightning storm,
    And viral phlegm's infectious swarm.

3.
Is life not filled enough with things like war?
The prodigal genius of humankind
    Confers renewed glamor
    Upon conflict and forever

Grants reason to summon it, finds
Solace in unfilled promises of power,
    Invention that leads to loss,
As if we're born for war and it for us,

A beast we breed for force, that champs the bit,
That smiles, and knows we cannot control it.

Dining with Representatives
of the Vatican Museum

What little may be told will be told
In a curve of Phrygian gold, Minoan seals
Of slender boys flicked in sun by bull horns;
A lithe lioness, stretched, ready to kill;

A Corinthian bronze helmet, gashed over
Haunted eye holes — a fiercely dented forehead —
Coins struck with frowns, a vessel's scorched ribcage,
Puzzling remains of each life and each age.

Ulysses Deriding Polyphemus

Turner

Smiling sadly with beer beneath a canopy
Of canaried gold and song, so much cold wind
Gone out into dark cove of oar and sail,
Embarked with ships and cries in high rigging.

After years, our storms relaxed, drew
Ink for blood: myth and life balanced at length,
Rescued from history by ruin, scrubbed yachts
Then scrapped hulks. Once we sat in sunshine,

But now we assemble in shadows,
Tarnished, recalling the years
Before our flight, in a field between armies.
Let us drink together as friends, freely.

I have no part of you, or you of me,
Passing our lives in peace as in war,
Just as what music survives acquires
Its territory from silence, so this.

She Who Was the Helmet-Maker's Beautiful Wife

All that's shaped is sheltered from chance,
And what's been saved may be sung.

Felon, old friend, death won't be away for long.
Remain with me a while in our snowy park.

Let's hear what is yet to come,
Warres in latter ages ended in darke.

6.

I did not see the monster, to my great regret — the great disappointment of my life, probably.
> — Edward Gorey, on his visit to Loch Ness

Independence Day

We wait for fireworks that never arrive.
The halfhearted breeze blows humidly
Around us on the beached old tug named Thor.
Before us dock the speedboat *I'm Alive*,
Skipjack *Ida May*, the trawler *Big Sea*.
The line between sea and land that makes the shore

Grows harder to see in the dusk. We
Watch the sore sun slip from bold orb to tiger
Stripe at the horizon with blue cloud rags
Dragged in the storm's wake. We talk, agree
The fireworks display might come soon, figure
We only need to wait a while more to see.

We lean back, and the cool coarse wood
Feels good, stare up at what's left of the day,
And then full dark, and, after half an hour,
When we know they will not come, that we could
Go if we wanted, for some reason we stay
There with *Miss May*, *Old Joy*, *Lady Flower*,

Olympia, *Lazee*, *One Love*, *Osprey*.
When we look away from the hollow
Dark above down to the darker harbor
And all the quivered light along the quay,
We see the black itself as a berth for the glow
Of masthead and stern lights on sloop and cutter,

Ketch and schooner, safe after the storm, dividing
Darkness, as if dreaming what seemed about
To happen, hulls of *Isabel, Edna, Ain't it Grand,*
Side by side in the indistinct tide, guiding
Bright quick ripples of surviving light that bear out
To meet us where we still wait on darkened land.

House and Home

1.
The raccoon is sinister, quick and silent,
With strange human hands and black mineral

Eyes that shine and seem to know me somehow.
She noses smoothly past feral cats

To get at the bowl of food we've left out.
Our cats watch patiently through the screen.

Birds drop from branches, swerving in squadrons.

2.
In the house, at night, I wait for a ghost
To present itself in the creaking halls.

Trains groan low and clatter across the meadow.
Refinery fires pulse on the river.

But no ghost, not yet. When I rise at night
For the bathroom, past the empty spare room,

I feel a boy's fingers, faint as snow, on my wrist.

Washington's Crossing

The railway bridge runs above the river's
Slow black, a stone Roman aqueduct,
Remnant of an age of commerce gone quiet.

I once stood on the soggy bank and saw
The river run low on a September day.
Now, snow still holds, and night's fallen.

The current is high and strong in the dark,
Tugging trunks toward the sea, bobbing
Roots spiking out from foam and swinging like antlers.

Time and Tide

The mountain's foot is soot in cloud shadow,
    But light drops cool stairways over the sea.
Sails rise like teeth on the horizon, slow
      Angles slanting and righting. I want to be
        Alone here. I want you to suffer. I do.
        I want those ships to burn. So do you.

Glacier

1.
At the timberline, the air, lush and cold,
Begins to thin in strumming rain.

We rip at white flukes of broiled chicken
Beside the abandoned mine, where the path

Splits. "When you take a first step, you must keep the path
To its end."

        Rivulets spin and hiss through slim crags,
Lured to oceans they'll reach many months from now.

A wet pain is still small in my new boots.
As we march, our fingers brush drops from lake-blue

Phosphoric match-heads of flax and larkspur.
Peaks score the fog like faint cathedral spires

Or sails confronting the dusk of a restless coast.

2.
My slower spirit lifts in a soft shower
As we gain the stony approach to the peak.
I start to hate the two rising above me,
Their lurching torsos lost amid the rocks.
I'm dragging like an anchor in their wake.

I stake my steps slowly, one, then one,
And imagine a procession where I must brake,
Hesitate, and advance in a kingly way,
Held back by custom rather than nature,
Though my stop-motion stance is not a king's
But a beggar's, burdened, abused in retreat.
Lady Gravity wants me at the bottom.

3.
Valleys plunge in squalls. Shadows lurk,
Spread over the dizzying view, a smeared rainbow
Arcing to incise luxuriant banks of fir.
Far below, aspen lines grin like baleen.
My lungs scald and gulp.
My veins punch hard — high-caliber and hot.
My soaked head bobs as if in a tide.

Rainwater decants effortlessly,
Glinting in slim mercury veins
Over gray granite scabs. Tiny trumpets
Speckle the bouldered ocean of green incline,
Tilted like a wave that swells and will take
A million years to break.
                              Summer thaws
Behind us. Above, murky Cretaceous monsters
Breach and loom, but we aim all afternoon
To their callous brunt, their ferocious slant,
Whale's barnacled snout, barren meadows
Of a brutal seafloor a million years ago.
What furnace abandoned this dark form?

4.

We arrive at the rim, where the glacier slips,
And gaze down. The glazed precipice
Opens an ancient scarred cavern in me.
It slows and molts, until a numb seep,
And I am suddenly softened,
Affection exhaled, and tranquility.
The others toe the high edge, pose like heroes
Over the vast bowl of ice and rain.
Did they defeat me? Was there a contest at all?
My subterranean core surges
Like the brass tablet of the sun,
Smoldering and nearer now, glowing through
The treacherous reaches of a receding storm.

White Horse

mons albi equi – an Abingdon cartulary, 1072-1084

Between trolley tracks, nestled in new concrete,
It strides in place: The White Horse,
Liquid stillness, its mane trailed softly
Like jellyfish in ocean current,
Its legs thin streams, tail fanned to a delta.

In a lush Vale near Oxford,
A chalk horse, a simpler form, kin,
Scratched white into the hard green,
An old equine specter escaping over scarp.

Someone must tend it or it would be
Consumed in a year by grass.
Nations wear away while it stays — with help
From those who returned age after age
Perhaps from simple habit, not knowing why.

In dark caves *horse* is simple glyph,
Smeared onto stone with charcoal and spit,
A creature forever untamable,
Always aimed urgently away from us
And what we dare to hope will remain.

Rain begins again. The outline sketched here
Is so light it almost eludes us.
Who put it here? A horn blasts
Me from a trance. I step to safety.
A trolley rumbles and clanks forward
Casting the horse beneath it into shadow.

Ocean Swimming

I float for years, it seems, toes out.
Small planes drone down the coast

To tow out ads for bars and bands or beer
As proud sea birds screech loud and strut

The black breakwaters that mark my circuit
To one jetty and then back to the first.

I roll into the cold, control
What I can in the wrestled element,

Appeal against a stronger surge,
Correct my forward course each stroke

To make a simple way that goes
Away as quickly as my wake,

Unwinnable struggle to stay afloat,
Small pulse of salt in endless salt.

7.

    . . . we have traced the stream
From darkness, and the very place of birth
In its blind cavern, whence is faintly heard
The sound of waters; followed it to light
And open day . . .
       — William Wordsworth, *The Prelude*, 1805,
       Book XIII

For Lynn, at Lackawanna

From the stillness a Green-tailed towhee
Slips from a cedar snag where the long lake curves
Away south. I aim our canoe at a glint of green
      On water black as fresh-cut coal:

A maple leaf, like a tiny crown, glows
On the surface. The bird begins to trill.
Waves bob the bright green leaf. Like love
      It rises and falls, yet stays near us.

Our child swims the warm star of your belly,
Ignited by a galaxy of nerves,
Nourished by a nebula of bloodstream,
      Sleek and simple as a tadpole.

We slow so we can see in murk below
Faint fingers of stargrass ripple and frill
As if feeling to find something above,
      As winds cross the cold lake to warm us.

Super Bowl Sunday

1.
On the blue couch the brown tabby cat
Curls content as a dragon on its hoard.

He claws lazily at a drift of junk mail,
Then lolls back on a lopsided pillow.

Beside him I hold you, not yet one,
My son, swaddled in butterflies.

You stretch, cheep like a finch,
Burble and plop open your wet mouth

Like a koi lapping at a leaf on a lake.
Squirrels skitter and startle each other outside.

You squirm on my lap this late sunny Saturday
In a cold month. This is enough. We abide.

I'm reading a wife's memoir of her husband,
A poet as sentimental as I, as foolish

And as easily made up of failures,
Sometimes as stupidly happy.

Don Giovanni roars, cast down
Into the depths of the black stereo.

2.
Soon the great game will commence.
Towering champions, created to win,

Will strut to their positions and pose,
Burnished, armored in emblems.

Lenses will zag and pan as the colors crash
And tumble all in a triumphal heap.

Already the light is leaving, and windows brighten
Across the street. In the edging dark,

Unsure, you imitate my smile in miniature,
Your first, not long held, but you will try again.

The world is deep with unwon battles,
Merciless and uncertain as our memories.

3.
I rise, cradling you, my son, carefully
Like a football in one arm as you yawn,

Grope with my free hand for the switch.
Your aquatic eyes give back the last of the light,

And a moment I myself seem slight and alive,
Restless and agile, the reckless lengths I ran

So long ago no longer gone, so long ago that day
When like you in lightning and rivers I began.

American Glass

I guide his stroller through a room that glows.
On every side, the glass is lit in rows.
He leans to see, his eyes grown big and flecked
With light, like water risen to a pool
From ancient aquifers, pupil and cool
Bright iris panes that fill as they reflect:
The summer ambers, peach, and arctic blues,
Crystal compotes that cradled cinnamon,
Citrus, cloves, and syrup, cut-glass jars
With cedar fragrances of Caribbean cigars,
Flint glass veined with daring spirals of cyclamen,
Gem-like decanters brimmed with burgundies,
Cruets like amphorae, ages past, suffused
With rich cologne of bitter orange and jasmine,
Trays that relayed whole empires of candies.
Fat-bottomed spoon holders and brown spittoons,
Votives rounded like seeds, pillars of whale-oil lamps,
Patriotic beakers, spangled big balloons
With presidents puffing chests in armed camps,
Green, muddy mugs that steamed with chicories,
Curled nautiluses perfumed in pink knots,
Ale glasses etched with wiry vines and leaves,
White butter dishes shaped as dreadnoughts,
Enchanted vessels made only to hold
The gruel, the wine and wind, the warmth and cold.

Fool's Fire

1.
Lights out. From bed
I look out the window, a bare

December view from
The crown of Squirrel Hill.

The moon's arctic cuticle
Points to our silver linden,

Its leaning silhouette
Gaunt and unleafed.

Burled limbs knot heavily,
Haunted by summers.

Through its dendritic reach of branch,
The gravel cutting of the SEPTA line,

The looming red-brick wreck
Of the HERMAN Iron Works,

Then the slow murk of the Schuylkill
At low tide, wind-rumpled mud flats,

Cemeteries asleep above the banks
And the unnavigable garbage bogs,

Bales of barbed wire and half-sunk strollers.

2.
Quick and bright, then faint,
Refinery gas flares

From the old Arco plant
Hover over the horizon,

Torches blustered by wind,
Their pent fuel phantomed into fire,

Spent in spectacular meteors
Up the black sky, Will-o'-the-wisps,

Like the legendary flickers that lured
Medieval pilgrims from well-worn ways

To roam frozen marshes
In search of Fairy Lights

That only recede until they fade,
Leaving them

Alone in darkness.

3.
I light my lamp, take up my book,
But the tiny type just junks to nothing,

So I look up for the distant fires.
There are none. I read. I look again

And there is one. Then two.
In summer, when the linden is full,

The ghost lights endure
Unseen beyond the green,

But in winter they summon
And bloom all night.

My wife and child dream, secure from gusts
That rattle the window pane

Above the antique radiator that ticks and sings
Under its unsteady stacks of unread books.

Such small comforts remain a while,
So why can I not keep myself

From watching for the far-off lights,
Meaning so much now and nothing,

Forever beckoning me from my bed?

Lesser Feasts

For Ian

The house is cold today, a deep-rooted fortress,
Foundation blocks of Wissahickon Schist,
Micah sparkling in late December sun,

A hull becalmed between two storms, iced recess
And an expectant clearness between mist
And sleet, as if a brief peace had been won.

For soup, I rend the Christmas turkey carcass,
Yank slick, sturdy strands apart, though some resist
My hands as jellied fat, warmed, begins to run.

The hard world yields little we may possess.
Our newborn opens and fastens his fist.
Happy, we sort a small steading for our son.

Year's end, and light's begun to dispossess
The exhausted dark. I trace his small wrist.
May life, like light, be strong before it's done.

The Author

Ernest Hilbert's debut poetry collection *Sixty Sonnets* (2009) was described by X.J. Kennedy as "maybe the most arresting sequence we have had since John Berryman checked out of America." His second collection, *All of You on the Good Earth* (2013), has been hailed as a "wonder of a book," "original and essential," an example of "sheer mastery of poetic form," containing "some of the most elegant poems in American literature since the loss of Anthony Hecht." His third collection, *Caligulan* (2015), has been called "brutal yet beautiful," defined by "pleasure, clarity, and discipline," "tough-minded and precise," filled with a "stern, witty, and often poignant music," "a page-turner in a way most poetry books can never be," and "an honest book for dishonest times." It was selected as winner of the 2017 Poets' Prize. Hilbert works as an antiquarian bookseller in Philadelphia, where he lives with his wife and their son, Ian.